SUCCESSFUL COOKING

MINCE

INDEX

Contents

Making Mince Fabulous

Mince is the most versatile, and economical, cut of meat available. It absorbs flavours and seasonings wonderfully and is used throughout the world in an incredible variety of dishes. It is mince that is enjoyed by a Greek family when they sit down to a hearty moussaka; mince that is stuffed into small rice dumplings by a Chinese chef in a busy dim sum restaurant; and mince that has been elevated almost to a national symbol in the all-American hamburger. With a little imagination, and a little help from this book, turn your everyday mince into something fabulous.

Although most people instantly think 'beef' when they think of mince, in fact the word 'mince' refers to any meat, fish or seafood that has been finely chopped.

Beef mince does deserve its pre-eminent position. It is by far the most easily available mince and its popularity means you should always have a choice of different grades. Pick the right cut for your recipe (see our tips below) and what you will be taking home is an economical form of what can be an expensive meat. Add some fresh vegetables or pulses, and even a small amount can grow into a meal for a large and hungry family.

Though beef mince may be the foundation of many of our favourite family recipes (and we've included many of those traditional classics inside), there are also lots of great recipes using other kinds of mince. Chicken and lamb are familiar, but pork and veal mince, prawn or even fish can bring a new flavour and texture to a family recipe. Or try using these minces to make something a little different. The Asian Lemon Grass Prawn Satays are deliciously light and only take about 20 minutes to prepare.

BUYING FROM YOUR BUTCHER

Most butchers stock a variety of different mince grades. Plain ground beef, often called hamburger, is a mixture of several beef cuts and can contain as much as 30 percent fat. (Look at the amount of white marbling in the meat, this is the fat, and the more there is, the fattier the meat is.) Hamburger is the least expensive kind of mince, but don't forget that its high fat content means it will shrink a lot when cooked. This grade of mince is therefore fine for dishes such as Lasagne but, despite its name, it's not the grade to choose if you want to make great hamburgers: your patties will just shrink too much when cooked. A leaner mince is ground chuck steak, which has around 20 percent fat. This is one of the best and most useful beef minces, with just enough fat to give flavour, but not so much that your patties and meatballs shrivel up when cooked. This is the mince to go for when you want to make juicy, flavourful hamburgers and, when our recipes ask for 'lean beef mince', this grade is a good choice. A ground sirloin is often labelled as extra lean and can contain half as much fat as ordinary ground beef. This is the perfect grade for those watching their diet, but it can dry out if cooked for too long.

For other minces, such as chicken or lamb, the cut of meat doesn't matter so much and the fat content is naturally lower. Just make sure with all minces that your meat is as fresh as possible, and don't keep it in the refrigerator for more than 2 days.

When considering all these new leaner minces, remember that mince does need some fat. It adds greatly to the flavour, keeps the meat tender and stops it drying out. A very lean cut will dry out quickly if cooked for a long time. If you want to cut down on fat and cholesterol, try recipes where the meat is browned first; then you can drain off much of the fat from the frying pan.

MINCING YOUR OWN

Beef, pork, lamb and chicken mince are usually readily available from a good butcher. But if you want to use an unusual cut of meat, fish or perhaps some shellfish, you will probably need to buy the meat or seafood and mince it yourself.

To mince your own meat, place the trimmed meat in a food processor and process in short bursts. The result will be a mince with a smooth texture—ideal for sausages or hamburgers. Alternatively, make your own mince by chopping a fillet of lean meat or fish with a large, sharp knife. This method works particularly well for tender cuts, such as a fresh fish fillet or a small amount of a prime beef cut such as rump.

Mincing your own meat or fish allows you a lot more choice. You can make sure that your mince is really fresh by picking the cut carefully at your butcher's and mincing it just before you want to use it. This also means that you can trim the sinew from your cut before you mince it. When you buy beef mince, the sinew has

BROWNING MINCE

Make sure you brown your mince in small batches so that it has a chance to cook and brown evenly, rather than stewing over the heat. As it cooks, break up any lumps to give the meat a better texture and appearance.

WORKING WITH MINCE MAKING PATTIES, MEATBALLS AND KOFTAS

When making patties, meatballs and koftas, it is important to make sure the meat is sticky enough to hold together well and keep its shape. However, you also want to prevent the meat becoming too compact, which means it will taste heavy when cooked. Follow the tips below to create light meatballs and patties that really work.

Mix together all the ingredients by hand. This helps the mince to come together and it will be less likely to fall apart during cooking.

You can mould the patties by hand or in egg rings. Wetting your hands first will make it easier to handle the meat.

When using skewers, mould the meat around the skewer, rather than threading it on. The meat will then stay together when cooked.

When you are grilling or cooking the patties, turn only once or twice, so that the meat doesn't dry out or fall apart.

sometimes been minced along with the rest of the meat and this is what can cause even finely ground mince to taste a little tough.

Another bonus of mincing your own is if you want to cut down onthe fat in your diet. It is often hard to tell how lean ready-made mince really is. Instead, buy your own cut of meat, trim the fat (remembering to leave enough to keep the meat moist and flavourful) and mince the meat yourself. This way you can get exactly the quality of meat and leanness that you want.

It also allows you to get a really fine mince. A coarse mince works well for most dishes and prevents the meat becoming too bruised. However, for some dishes, such as meatballs and terrines, you need a really fine mince, which will hold together well and keep its shape better when cooked. If you have bought ready-made mince, you can chop it again at home to give it this finer texture.

Process in small bursts until the meat has the texture of mince.

To make your own mince, place chunks of the meat into a food processor.

Alternatively, use a sharp knife to chop the meat by hand.

Beef Pie

PREPARATION TIME:
35 minutes + 30 minutes refrigeration
TOTAL COOKING TIME: 1 hour
SERVES 6

¾ cup (90 g/3 oz) plain flour
⅓ cup (40 g/1⅓ oz) self-raising flour
90 g (3 oz) butter, chopped
2 rashers rindless bacon, chopped
1 small onion, finely chopped
750 g (1½ lb) lean beef mince
2 tablespoons plain flour, extra
1½ cups (375 ml/12 fl oz) beef stock
½ cup (125 g/4 oz) tomato paste
2 tablespoons Worcestershire sauce
2 teaspoons dried mixed herbs
1 tablespoon dry mustard
375 g (12 oz) block frozen puff pastry
1 egg, lightly beaten

1 Mix the flours and butter in a food processor until fine and crumbly. Add 1 tablespoon of water and process until the mixture comes together, adding more water if necessary. Turn out onto a floured surface and gather it into a ball. Cover with plastic wrap and refrigerate for 30 minutes. Roll the pastry on a sheet of baking paper until large enough to cover the base and sides of a greased 23 cm (9 inch) round pie dish and refrigerate.

2 Heat some oil in a pan and cook the bacon and onion for 5 minutes. Add the beef mince and cook for 4 minutes, or until the liquid has evaporated and the meat browned. Use a fork to break up any lumps of mince as it cooks. Stir in the flour for 1 minute.

3 Add the stock, paste, sauce, herbs and mustard and bring to the boil. Reduce the heat and simmer, stirring occasionally, for 8 minutes, or until most of the liquid has evaporated. Cool, then place in the pastry shell. Preheat the oven to hot 210°C (415°F/Gas 6–7).

4 On a floured surface, roll out the puff pastry until it is large enough to cover the pie. Brush the edge of the pie shell with egg, place the pastry on top and trim the edges. Make cuts around the edge, cutting right through the pastry, and 4 cuts in the top. Brush with egg. Bake for 15 minutes. Reduce the heat to moderate 180°C (350°F/Gas 4) and bake for 25 minutes, or until golden.

Process the flours and butter until fine and crumbly.

Add the stock, tomato paste, sauce, herbs and mustard to the meat.

Nachos

PREPARATION TIME: 30 minutes
TOTAL COOKING TIME: 25 minutes
SERVES 4

400 g (12⅔ oz) lean beef mince
1 onion, chopped
1–2 teaspoons chopped fresh chilli
1 tablespoon ground cumin
3 teaspoons ground coriander
¼ cup (60 g/2 oz) tomato paste
½ cup (125 g/4 oz) ready-made tomato
  pasta sauce or salsa
½ cup (115 g/ 3¾ oz) refried beans or 425 g
  (13½ oz) can red kidney beans, drained
corn chips, grated Cheddar cheese and sour
  cream, for serving

Guacamole
1 ripe avocado
1 small onion, finely chopped
1 tomato, finely chopped
2 tablespoons chopped fresh coriander
2–3 tablespoons sour cream
3–4 teaspoons lemon juice
Tabasco, to taste

1 Heat a little oil in a frying pan and brown the beef mince in batches, stirring and breaking up any lumps with a fork or wooden spoon. Transfer to a bowl and set aside.

2 Add a little more oil to the pan and stir in the onion, chilli, cumin and coriander. Cook over medium heat for 2–3 minutes. Return the mince to the pan and stir in the tomato paste and sauce and refried or kidney beans. Simmer for 5–10 minutes.

3 To make Guacamole: Peel the avocado and mash the flesh in a bowl. Add the onion, tomato, coriander, sour cream and lemon juice. Mix well with a fork. Add some salt, freshly ground black pepper and Tabasco.

4 Spoon the mince into a large, ovenproof dish. Arrange the corn chips around the mixture and sprinkle with the cheese. Place under a preheated grill or in a moderate 180°C (350°F/Gas 4) oven for about 5–10 minutes, or until the cheese has melted. Top with the Guacamole, a spoonful of sour cream and a dash of chilli powder.

Break up any lumps of mince with a fork or wooden spoon.

Stir in the tomato paste and sauce and the refried beans.

Add the onion, tomato, coriander, sour cream and lemon juice to the avocado.

Hamburger with The Works

PREPARATION TIME: 20 minutes

TOTAL COOKING TIME: 15 minutes

SERVES 4

500 g (1 lb) lean beef mince
1 onion, finely chopped
1 egg, lightly beaten
⅓ cup (25 g / ¾ oz) fresh breadcrumbs
2 tablespoons tomato sauce
1 teaspoon steak seasoning
40 g (1⅓ oz) butter
2 onions, extra, cut in thin rings
4 slices Cheddar cheese, halved
4 eggs, extra
4 slices rindless bacon, halved
4 large hamburger buns, halved
shredded lettuce
1 large tomato, sliced
4 large beetroot slices, drained
4 pineapple rings, drained
tomato sauce, for serving

1 Place the beef mince, onion, egg, breadcrumbs, tomato sauce, steak seasoning and some salt and pepper in a large bowl. Use your hands to mix well. Divide into 4 portions and shape into round patties. Heat 30 g (1 oz) butter in a frying pan, add the onion rings and cook over medium heat until brown. Remove and keep warm.

2 Heat a frying pan or barbecue grill or flatplate and brush lightly with oil. Cook the patties for 3–4 minutes each side, or until cooked through. Place a cheese slice on each patty.

3 While the patties are cooking, heat the remaining butter in another frying pan and fry the eggs and the bacon separately. Toast the buns and top each one with lettuce, tomato, beetroot and pineapple. Add a meat patty and finish with some onion, egg and bacon.

Use your hands to mix the mince with the other ingredients.

Cook the patties for 3–4 minutes each side, or until cooked through.

Cook the bacon in a non-stick pan until it is crisp. Turn it over frequently.

Sausage Rolls

PREPARATION TIME: 40 minutes

TOTAL COOKING TIME: 35 minutes

MAKES 8

150 g (4 ¾ oz) sausage mince
150 g (4 ¾ oz) lean beef mince
1 small onion, finely chopped or grated
2 eggs
1–2 cloves garlic, crushed
1 tablespoon barbecue sauce
3 teaspoons Worcestershire sauce
½ cup (40 g/1⅓ oz) fresh breadcrumbs
2–3 tablespoons finely chopped fresh parsley
2 sheets ready-rolled puff pastry
tomato or chilli sauce, for serving

1 Preheat the oven to moderate 180°C (350°F/Gas 4). Line 2 baking trays with non-stick baking paper.

2 Using your hands, mix together the sausage and beef minces, onion, 1 egg, garlic, sauces, breadcrumbs, parsley and some salt and pepper.

3 Cut the pastry sheets in half and brush lightly with some of the remaining beaten egg. Divide the mince mixture into 4 equal portions and place 1 portion in a long sausage shape down the centre of each sheet.

4 Roll the pastry over the mixture and press the edges to seal, leaving the ends open. Use a sharp knife to cut the sausage rolls in half, then place on the trays, seam-side-down, ensuring there is enough room for them to spread. Brush with egg and lightly score the tops diagonally with a sharp knife. Bake for 35 minutes, or until crisp and golden. Serve with tomato or chilli sauce.

Variation: Lightly sprinkle the rolls with poppy or sesame seeds after glazing with egg and before baking.

Combine the minces, onion, 1 egg, garlic, sauces, breadcrumbs and parsley.

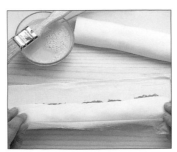
Carefully roll the pastry over the mixture and press the edges to seal.

Score the tops diagonally, being careful not to cut right through the pastry.

15

Chicken and Lemon Meatballs

PREPARATION TIME:
20 minutes + 30 minutes refrigeration
TOTAL COOKING TIME: 10 minutes
SERVES 4

500 g (1 lb) chicken mince
2 cloves garlic, crushed
1 cup (80 g/2⅔ oz) fresh white breadcrumbs
1 teaspoon grated lemon rind
1 teaspoon fresh lemon thyme leaves
1 egg, lightly beaten
1 tablespoon olive oil
2 tablespoons lemon juice

Yoghurt Mint Sauce
200 g (6½ oz) plain yoghurt
1 tablespoon shredded fresh mint
rinsed, chopped skin from ¼ of a
    preserved lemon

1 Using your hands, mix together the chicken mince, garlic, breadcrumbs, lemon rind, thyme, egg and some salt and black pepper. Wet your hands and form tablespoons of the mixture into balls and place on a lined tray. Refrigerate for 30 minutes.

2 To make Yoghurt Mint Sauce: Mix together all the ingredients.

3 Heat the oil in a non-stick frying pan and cook the meatballs in 2 batches, until golden on all sides and cooked through. Sprinkle with lemon juice, transfer to a serving dish and sprinkle with more salt. Serve with Yoghurt Mint Sauce.

Combine the chicken, garlic, breadcrumbs, lemon rind, thyme, egg, salt and pepper.

Using wet hands, roll tablespoons of the mixture into balls.

Cook the meatballs in batches until golden and cooked through.

Shepherd's Pie

PREPARATION TIME: 30 minutes
TOTAL COOKING TIME: 1 hour
SERVES 4–6

750 g (1½ lb) lean cooked lamb
25 g (¾ oz) butter
2 onions, thinly sliced
¼ cup (30 g/1 oz) plain flour
½ teaspoon dry mustard
1½ cups (375 ml/12 fl oz) chicken stock
2 tablespoons chopped fresh mint
1 tablespoon chopped fresh parsley
2 tablespoons Worcestershire sauce

Potato Topping
4 large potatoes, cooked
¼ cup (60 ml/2 fl oz) hot milk
30 g (1 oz) butter

1 Brush an 8-cup capacity ovenproof dish with melted butter or oil. Preheat the oven to hot 210°C (415°F/Gas 6–7). Trim the meat and mince finely with a sharp knife. Melt the butter in a pan, add the onion and cook until brown. Sprinkle with flour and mustard.

2 Gradually add the stock and stir until smooth. Bring to the boil, reduce the heat and simmer for 3 minutes. Stir in the lamb mince, mint, parsley, Worcestershire sauce and some salt and black pepper. Spoon the mixture into the dish.

3 To make Potato Topping: Mash the potatoes slightly and then add the milk, butter and some salt and pepper. Mash until the potato is smooth and creamy, adding more milk if necessary. Pipe or spread over the meat and bake for 40–45 minutes, or until the potato is golden.

Using a sharp knife, finely chop the lean cooked lamb until minced.

Gradually add the stock and stir with a wooden spoon until smooth.

Mash the potatoes and mix with the milk, butter, salt and pepper until smooth.

Rissoles with Gravy

PREPARATION TIME: 40 minutes
TOTAL COOKING TIME: 15–20 minutes
MAKES 10

500 g (1 lb) lean beef mince
1 onion, finely chopped
2 cloves garlic, crushed
2 tablespoons tomato paste or sauce
2–3 teaspoons Dijon mustard
2 tablespoons chopped fresh parsley
1 tablespoon chopped fresh lemon thyme
  or chives
2 eggs
flour, for dusting
milk
1 cup (100 g/3⅓ oz) dried breadcrumbs

Gravy
1 tablespoon plain flour
1 cup (250 ml/8 fl oz) beef or vegetable stock
¼ cup (60 ml/2 fl oz) red wine

1 Using your hands, combine the beef mince, onion, garlic, tomato paste or sauce, mustard, herbs and 1 beaten egg in a large bowl. Season with salt and freshly ground black pepper. Shape into patties by pressing small handfuls of the mixture into floured egg rings. Press down with your hand to flatten the patties, then remove the egg ring and lightly dust each patty with flour.

2 Whisk the remaining egg with a little milk. Dip the patties, one at a time, into the egg mixture and then coat in breadcrumbs, gently pressing so that the breadcrumbs stick. Heat a little oil in a large frying pan. Cook the rissoles in batches, over medium heat, for 3–4 minutes each side, or until cooked through and well browned. Remove from the pan, cover and keep warm.

3 To make Gravy: Drain any excess oil from the pan, leaving about 2–3 teaspoons. Add the flour and stir for 1 minute. Gradually blend in the combined stock and red wine, stirring to incorporate the bits from the base of the pan. Stir constantly, over medium heat, until the sauce boils and thickens. Simmer for 2–3 minutes and season with salt and pepper. Pour the gravy over the rissoles and serve.

Shape into patties by pressing small amounts of mixture into floured egg rings.

Dip each patty into the egg and then press into the breadcrumbs.

Spicy Lamb Curry

PREPARATION TIME: 30 minutes

TOTAL COOKING TIME: 40 minutes

SERVES 4

750 g (1½ lb) lean lamb mince
1 tablespoon soy sauce
2 tablespoons chopped fresh coriander
2 tablespoons oil
2 large onions, sliced
2 teaspoons grated fresh ginger
2 garlic cloves, crushed
2 red chillies, chopped
6 curry leaves
1 teaspoon ground cinnamon
2 teaspoons ground turmeric
2 teaspoons grated lemon rind
1 tablespoon tamarind sauce
1 tablespoon white vinegar
3 tablespoons fruit or mango chutney
1½ cups (375 ml/12 fl oz) water

1 Mix together the lamb mince, soy sauce and coriander. Roll tablespoons of the mixture into balls. Heat the oil in a heavy-based frying pan. Cook the lamb balls, in batches, over medium heat for 4 minutes, or until brown, turning occasionally. Remove and drain on paper towels.

2 Add the onion, ginger, garlic and chilli to the pan and stir-fry over medium heat for 2 minutes, or until the onion is tender.

3 Add the curry leaves, cinnamon, turmeric, lemon rind, tamarind sauce, vinegar, chutney and water to the pan; bring to the boil. Return the lamb meatballs to the pan, reduce the heat and simmer, covered, for 15 minutes, or until the sauce has reduced and thickened, stirring occasionally.

Note: Make this curry up to 2 days in advance for the flavours to develop. Store, covered, in the refrigerator.

Remove the meatballs from the pan and drain on paper towels.

Stir the onions over medium heat until they are tender.

Add curry leaves, spices, lemon rind, tamarind, vinegar, chutney and water.

Savoury Mince

PREPARATION TIME: 25 minutes
TOTAL COOKING TIME: 25 minutes
SERVES 4–6

3 tablespoons oil
30 g (1 oz) butter
500 g (1 lb) lean beef mince
1 onion, chopped
1 large carrot, grated
⅓ cup (80 ml/2¾ fl oz) tomato sauce
⅓ cup (80 ml/2¾ fl oz) beef or vegetable stock
2 teaspoons Dijon or English mustard
2 tablespoons chopped fresh parsley
1–2 cloves garlic, crushed
crusty bread slices

1 Heat about 2 teaspoons of the oil and half the butter in a large frying pan. Add the beef mince in batches and stir constantly, over high heat, until well browned, breaking up any lumps with a fork or wooden spoon. Transfer the mince to a bowl and set aside.

2 Add the remaining butter and 2 teaspoons of oil to the pan. Stir in the onion and cook over medium heat for 3–4 minutes, or until golden.

3 Return the meat to the pan and stir in the carrot, tomato sauce, stock and mustard. Reduce the heat and simmer the sauce for 5–10 minutes, or until the liquid has reduced and the sauce thickened. Stir in the parsley and season, to taste, with salt and freshly ground black pepper.

4 Combine the remaining oil with the crushed garlic and brush over each slice of bread. Place the bread under a preheated grill and toast each side until golden. Spoon the mince over the toast and serve.

Use a wooden spoon or fork to break up any lumps of meat.

Stir the onion over medium heat until it turns golden.

Simmer until the liquid reduces and the sauce has thickened.

Pizza with Red Capsicum and Beef

PREPARATION TIME: 35 minutes

TOTAL COOKING TIME: 30 minutes

SERVES 2–4

1 small red capsicum
1 large ready-madepizza base
2–3 tablespoons tomato paste
1 clove garlic, crushed
½ teaspoon sweet paprika
1 red onion, thinly sliced
1 teaspoon olive oil
125 g (4 oz) lean beef mince
10 Kalamata olives, pitted and
   roughly chopped
1 tablespoon fresh oregano leaves
1 fresh red chilli, finely sliced
1 cup (150 g/4¾ oz) grated mozzarella cheese

1 Cut the capsicum into large pieces, removing the seeds and membrane and brush the skin lightly with some oil. Grill, skin-side-up, until the skin blisters and blackens. Seal in a plastic bag, or cover with a damp tea towel, until cool. Remove the skin and slice the flesh thinly.

2 Preheat the oven to moderately hot 200°C (400°F/Gas 6). Place the pizza base on a baking tray and spread with the combined tomato paste, garlic and paprika. Sprinkle with the red capsicum and onion.

3 Heat the oil in a frying pan and brown the beef mince well, breaking up any lumps with a fork or wooden spoon. Season with some salt and freshly ground black pepper.

4 Sprinkle the beef over the pizza and scatter with the olives, oregano leaves and chilli. Top with the mozzarella. Bake for 20 minutes, or until the base is crisp and the cheese has melted. Cut into wedges to serve.

Remove the seeds and membrane from the capsicum.

Combine the tomato paste, garlic and paprika and spread over the pizza base.

Sprinkle the beef over the top of the red capsicum and onion.

Tandoori Chicken Terrine

PREPARATION TIME:
20 minutes + overnight refrigeration
TOTAL COOKING TIME: 1 hour 30 minutes
SERVES 6–8

8 slices bacon, rind removed
30 g (1 oz) butter
1 medium onion, finely chopped
2 cloves garlic, crushed
1 teaspoon grated fresh ginger
1 kg (2 lb) chicken mince
250 g (8 oz) chicken livers
1 teaspoon turmeric
1 teaspoon sweet paprika
1 teaspoon garam masala
½ teaspoon ground cardamom
1 teaspoon ground coriander
2 tablespoons lemon juice
1 cup (250 g/8 oz) plain yoghurt
2 eggs, lightly beaten

1 Preheat the oven to moderate 180°C (350°F/Gas 4). Lightly oil a 27 x 10 cm (11 x 4 inch) terrine dish or tin and line with bacon, overlapping the sides of the dish. Melt the butter in a pan, add the onion, garlic and ginger and fry for 2–3 minutes. Remove from heat.

2 Finely mince the chicken mince and livers in a food processor. Transfer to a large bowl and add the onion mixture, spices and lemon juice.

3 Whisk the yoghurt and eggs and stir into the chicken mixture. Spoon into the dish, pressing down firmly. Fold the bacon over the top of the terrine to enclose the mixture, cover with foil and place in a baking dish.

4 Pour in enough cold water to come halfway up the terrine's sides. Bake for 1–1½ hours, or until the juices run clear when pierced with a skewer.

5 Remove from the oven and water bath and pour off the excess juice. Cover with foil and place a heavy weight on top of the terrine mixture to compress it. Refrigerate overnight.

Line the dish with bacon, leaving the ends overlapping the sides of the dish.

Spread the chicken mixture over the bacon, pressing down firmly.

Pour in enough cold water to come halfway up the sides of the terrine dish.

29

Meatball Stroganoff

PREPARATION TIME: 40 minutes
TOTAL COOKING TIME: 20–25 minutes
SERVES 4

750 g (1½ lb) lean beef mince
2 cloves garlic, crushed
2–3 tablespoons plain flour
½ teaspoon ground black pepper
1 teaspoon sweet paprika
2 tablespoons oil
50 g (1⅔ oz) butter
1 large onion, thinly sliced
250 g (8 oz) small button mushrooms, halved
2 tablespoons tomato paste
2–3 teaspoons Dijon mustard
¼ cup (60 ml/2 fl oz) white wine
½ cup (125 ml/4 fl oz) beef stock
¾ cup (185 g/6 oz) sour cream
3 tablespoons finely chopped fresh parsley

1 Combine the beef mince, garlic and some salt and cracked pepper in a bowl. Use your hands to mix well. Roll 2 heaped teaspoons of the mince into balls. Combine the flour, pepper and paprika on a clean surface or sheet of greaseproof paper. Dust the meatballs in the seasoned flour.

2 Heat the oil and half the butter in a frying pan. When foaming, cook the meatballs over medium heat, in batches, until brown. Remove from the pan and drain on paper towels.

3 Melt the remaining butter in the pan and add the onion. Cook for 2–3 minutes, or until soft. Stir in the mushrooms and continue cooking until the mushrooms are tender. Pour in the combined tomato paste, mustard, wine and stock. Return the meatballs to the pan and gently reheat. Bring the mixture to the boil, reduce the heat and simmer for 5 minutes, stirring occasionally. Season to taste with salt and pepper. Stir the sour cream through until smooth. Sprinkle over a little parsley and serve with noodles.

Roll the meatballs in the flour mixture until lightly coated.

Brown the meatballs in batches so that they fry rather than stew.

Pour in the combined tomato paste, mustard, wine and stock.

Herb and Onion Burger

PREPARATION TIME: 35 minutes

TOTAL COOKING TIME: 10–15 minutes

SERVES 4

400 g (12⅔ oz) lean beef mince
350 g (11¼ oz) pork and veal mince
1 tablespoon barbecue sauce
1 small red onion, finely chopped
3 teaspoons chopped fresh parsley
3 teaspoons chopped fresh oregano
3 teaspoons chopped chives
1 tablespoon chopped fresh mint
30 g (1 oz) butter
6 large bulb spring onions, sliced into rings
4 long crusty rolls, halved and lightly toasted
125 g (4 oz) Camembert cheese, thinly sliced

1 Combine the minces, barbecue sauce, onion, herbs and some salt and pepper in a large bowl, mixing well with your hands. Divide the mixture into 4 portions and shape them into long patties.

2 Heat a frying pan or grillplate and brush liberally with oil. Cook the patties in batches for 3–4 minutes each side, or until browned and cooked through. When they are almost cooked, heat the butter in a pan, add the spring onion and cook over medium heat until wilted.

3 Place the bases of the bread rolls on serving plates. Top each with a meat patty, cheese slices, spring onion and a few oregano sprigs. Cover with the roll tops and serve with your favourite sauce or relish.

Cut the spring onion bulbs into thin rings, discarding the green tops.

Combine the minces, salt, pepper, barbecue sauce, onion and herbs.

Cook the prepared patties in batches until browned and cooked through.

Chilli Con Carne

PREPARATION TIME: 15 minutes
TOTAL COOKING TIME: 55 minutes
SERVES 4

1 tablespoon olive oil
1 onion, chopped
3 cloves garlic, crushed
1 celery stick, sliced
500 g (1 lb) lean beef mince
2 teaspoons chilli powder
pinch of cayenne pepper
1 teaspoon dried oregano
425 g (13½ oz) can crushed tomatoes
2 tablespoons tomato paste
1 teaspoon soft brown sugar
1 tablespoon cider vinegar or red
  wine vinegar
420 g (13⅓ oz) can red kidney beans, rinsed
  and drained

1 Heat the oil in a large, heavy-based frying pan. Add the onion, garlic and celery and stir for 5 minutes, or until softened. Add the beef mince and stir over high heat for 5 minutes, or until well browned, breaking up any lumps with a fork or wooden spoon.

2 Add the chilli powder, cayenne pepper and oregano to the frying pan. Stir well and cook over medium heat for another 5 minutes. Add the tomatoes, ½ cup (125 ml/4 fl oz) water and the tomato paste and stir well. Simmer for 30 minutes, stirring occasionally.

3 Add the sugar, vinegar, drained beans and some salt and freshly ground black pepper to the pan and cook for 5 minutes. Serve hot with white or brown rice.

Storage time: Can be stored, covered and refrigerated, for up to 3 days.
Hint: Add more or less chilli powder, to taste. For a spicier dish, add some chopped fresh red chillies when you are cooking the onions.
Variation: If you prefer, you can use dried kidney beans in place of the canned variety. Place 250 g (8 oz) dried kidney beans in a large bowl and fill with water. Leave to soak overnight. Drain and place in a large pan, cover with water and cook for 35 minutes, or until just tender. Add the beans to the chilli at the same time as you would add the canned beans.

Add the chilli powder, cayenne and dried oregano to the meat and stir well.

Stir in the crushed tomatoes, water and tomato paste.

Won Ton Soup

PREPARATION TIME:
15 minutes+ 30 minutes soaking
TOTAL COOKING TIME: 20 minutes
SERVES 6

3 dried Chinese mushrooms
125 g (4 oz) pork mince
60 g (2 oz) raw prawn meat, finely chopped
½ teaspoon salt
2 teaspoons soy sauce
1 teaspoon sesame oil
1 spring onion, finely chopped
1 teaspoon grated fresh ginger
1 tablespoon finely chopped water chestnuts
24 won ton wrappers
1.25 litres chicken stock
4 spring onions, very finely sliced, to garnish

1 Soak the mushrooms in hot water for 30 minutes. Drain, then squeeze out the excess moisture. Remove the stems, chop the caps finely and mix with the pork mince, prawn meat, salt, soy sauce, oil, spring onion, ginger and water chestnuts.

2 Work with 1 won ton wrapper at a time, keeping the rest covered with a tea towel. Place 1 teaspoon of the mixture on each wrapper, then moisten the edges and bring the sides up to form a pouch.

3 Cook, in batches, in a pan of boiling water for 4–5 minutes. Remove and drain. Boil the stock in a pan. Place the won tons in bowls, garnish with spring onion and pour over the stock.

Remove the stems from the moist mushrooms and chop the caps.

Measure 1 teaspoon of the mixture onto each won ton wrapper.

Fold the wrapper up around the filling, to form a pouch.

Moussaka

PREPARATION TIME: 20 minutes + 1 hour standing
TOTAL COOKING TIME: 1 hour 45 minutes
SERVES 6

3 medium eggplants
½ cup (125 ml/4 fl oz) olive oil

Mince Sauce
2 tablespoons olive oil
1 large onion, finely chopped
500 g (1 lb) lean beef mince
2 tablespoons dry white wine
425 g (13½ oz) can tomato purée
1 tablespoon finely chopped fresh
   flat-leaf parsley
2 teaspoons finely chopped fresh mint leaves
½ teaspoon ground cinnamon

Cheese Sauce
90 g (3 oz) butter
⅓ cup (40 g/1⅓ oz) plain flour
2 cups (500 ml/16 fl oz) milk
2 eggs, lightly beaten
⅔ cup (85 g/2¾ oz) freshly grated
   Romano cheese

1 Cut the unpeeled eggplants into 1 cm (½ inch) slices. Sprinkle both sides with salt and leave in a colander for 1 hour. Rinse under cold water, then drain well. Squeeze out any excess moisture with paper towels.

2 To make Mince Sauce: Heat the oil in a pan. Add the onion and mince and stir over high heat for 10 minutes, or until the meat is well browned and all the liquid has evaporated. Add the wine, tomato purée, herbs, cinnamon and some white pepper and bring to the boil. Reduce heat and simmer, covered, for 20 minutes, stirring occasionally. Remove the lid and simmer for 10 minutes.

3 To make Cheese Sauce: Heat the butter in a small pan until foaming and then stir in the flour over low heat for 2 minutes. Add the milk gradually, stirring until smooth. Stir over medium heat for 5 minutes, or until the mixture boils and thickens. Cook for 1 minute, then remove from the heat. Add the eggs and cheese and beat until smooth.

4 Preheat the oven to moderate 180°C (350°F/Gas 4). Heat the oil in a heavy-based pan and cook the eggplant slices, a few at a time, until golden. Remove and drain on paper towels. Place a third of the eggplant in a shallow ovenproof dish. Cover with half the Mince Sauce, a layer of eggplant, and then another layer of each. Spread Cheese Sauce over the top layer of eggplant. Bake for 45 minutes, or until golden. Leave in the dish for 5 minutes before serving.

Sprinkle both sides of the eggplant slices with salt.

Stir the meat over high heat until all the liquid has evaporated.

San Choy Bau

PREPARATION TIME: 20 minutes
TOTAL COOKING TIME: 10 minutes
SERVES 2–4

1 tablespoon peanut oil
1 teaspoon sesame oil
1–2 cloves garlic, crushed
1 tablespoon grated fresh ginger
4 spring onions, chopped
500 g (1 lb) lean pork mince
1 red capsicum, seeded and finely diced
230 g (7⅓ oz) can water chestnuts, drained
  and roughly chopped
1–2 tablespoons soy sauce
1 tablespoon oyster sauce
2 tablespoons dry sherry
1 iceberg or butter lettuce

1 Heat the oils in a large, non-stick frying pan or wok. Add the garlic, ginger and spring onion and stir for about 2 minutes. Add the pork mince and cook over medium heat until well browned, breaking up any lumps with a fork or wooden spoon.

2 Stir in the capsicum, chestnuts, soy and oyster sauces and sherry. Simmer over medium heat until the liquid reduces and thickens. Keep warm.

3 Wash the lettuce and separate the whole leaves. Shake off the excess water. Place the lettuce cups on a plate and spoon in some pork mixture.

Note: You can also serve the lettuce leaves and pork mixture separately. Let everybody fill their own lettuce leaf with the pork, wrapping the lettuce around to form a package to hold with their fingers.

Drain the can of water chestnuts and roughly chop them.

Add the garlic, ginger and spring onion to the wok and stir for about 2 minutes.

Stir in the capsicum, water chestnuts, soy and oyster sauces and sherry.

41

Thai Fish Cakes

PREPARATION TIME: 25 minutes
TOTAL COOKING TIME: 10 minutes
SERVES 4–6

450 g (14⅓ oz) firm white fish fillets
3 tablespoons cornflour
1 tablespoon fish sauce
1 egg, beaten
½ cup (15 g/½ oz) fresh coriander leaves
1–2 teaspoons chopped red chilli, optional
3 teaspoons red curry paste
100 g (3⅓ oz) green beans, very finely sliced
2 spring onions, finely chopped
½ cup (125 ml/4 fl oz) oil
sweet chilli sauce, to serve

1 Process the fish in a food processor for 20 seconds, or until smooth. Add the cornflour, fish sauce, beaten egg, coriander leaves, red chilli and curry paste. Process for 10 seconds, or until well combined.

2 Transfer the fish mixture to a large bowl. Add the beans and spring onion and mix well. Using wet hands, form 2 tablespoons of the mixture at a time into flattish patties.

3 Heat the oil in a heavy-based frying pan over medium heat. Cook 4 fish cakes at a time until golden brown on both sides. Drain on paper towels and serve immediately with some sweet chilli sauce.

Storage time: You can prepare the fish cakes up to 4 hours in advance. After forming into patties, cover them lightly with plastic wrap and store in the refrigerator until you are ready to use them.

Add the cornflour, fish sauce, egg, coriander, paste and chilli.

Form 2 rounded tablespoons of the mixture at a time into flattish patties.

Cook the fish cakes in oil, until golden on both sides.

Spring Rolls

PREPARATION TIME: 40 minutes
TOTAL COOKING TIME: 20–25 minutes
MAKES 18

2 tablespoons oil
2 cloves garlic, chopped
3 cm (1¼ inch) piece of fresh ginger, grated
100 g (3⅓ oz) lean pork mince
100 g (3⅓ oz) chicken mince
50 g (1⅔ oz) raw prawns, minced
2 celery sticks, finely sliced
1 small carrot, finely chopped
½ cup (90 g/3 oz) chopped water chestnuts
4 spring onions, chopped
1 cup (75 g/2½ oz) finely shredded cabbage
½ cup (125 ml/4 fl oz) chicken stock
4 tablespoons cornflour
2 tablespoons oyster sauce
1 tablespoon soy sauce
2 teaspoons sesame oil
⅓ cup (80 ml/2¾ fl oz) water
36 spring roll wrappers
3 cups (750 ml/24 fl oz) oil
sweet chilli sauce, for serving

1 Heat 1 tablespoon oil in a wok or pan and cook the garlic and ginger for 30 seconds. Add the pork, chicken and prawn minces and cook for 3 minutes, or until the minces are brown. Transfer to a bowl.

2 Wipe the pan, then heat the remaining tablespoon of oil and add the celery, carrot, water chestnuts, spring onion and cabbage. Stir over medium heat for 2 minutes. Combine the chicken stock, 1 tablespoon cornflour, oyster and soy sauces and salt and pepper, add to the vegetables and stir until thickened. Stir the sesame oil and vegetables into the meat mixture and cool. Mix the remaining cornflour with the water until smooth.

3 Place 1 small square spring roll wrapper on the bench with a corner towards you. Brush all the edges with a little cornflour paste and cover with another wrapper. Brush the edges of the second wrapper and spread about 1½ tablespoons of the filling across the bottom corner of the wrapper. Fold the bottom corner up over the filling, fold in the sides and roll up firmly. Repeat with the remaining wrappers and filling. Heat the oil in a deep pan and fry the rolls, in batches, for 2–3 minutes, or until golden. Drain and serve with sweet chilli sauce.

Add the pork, chicken and prawn minces to the wok or pan and fry until brown.

Fold the bottom corner over the filling and fold in the sides before rolling up.

Indian Seekh Kebabs

PREPARATION TIME: 40 minutes
TOTAL COOKING TIME: 12 minutes
SERVES 4

pinch of ground cloves
pinch of ground nutmeg
½ teaspoon chilli powder
1 teaspoon ground cumin
2 teaspoons ground coriander
3 cloves garlic, finely chopped
5 cm (2 inch) piece of fresh ginger, grated
500 g (1 lb) lean beef mince
1 tablespoon oil
2 tablespoons lemon juice

Onion and Mint Relish
1 red onion, finely chopped
1 tablespoon white vinegar
1 tablespoon lemon juice
1 tablespoon chopped fresh mint

1 Soak 12 thick wooden skewers in cold water for 15 minutes. Dry-fry the cloves, nutmeg, chilli, cumin and coriander in a heavy-based frying pan, over low heat, for about 2 minutes, shaking the pan constantly. Transfer to a bowl with the garlic and ginger and set aside.

2 Knead the mince firmly using your fingertips and the base of your hand. The meat needs to be kneaded constantly for about 3 minutes, or until it becomes very soft and a little sticky. This process changes the texture of the meat when cooked, making it very soft and tender. Add the mince to the spice and garlic mixture and mix well, seasoning with plenty of salt and pepper.

3 Form tablespoons of the meat into small, round patty shapes. Wet your hands and press 2 portions of the meat around a skewer, leaving a gap of about 3 cm (1¼ inches) at the top of the skewer. Smooth the outside gently, place on baking paper and refrigerate while making the remaining kebabs.

4 To make Onion and Mint Relish: Combine the onion, vinegar and lemon juice in a small bowl; refrigerate for 10 minutes. Stir in the mint and season with pepper, to taste, just before serving.

5 Brush a preheated grill or hotplate with the oil. Grill the skewers for about 8 minutes, turning regularly and sprinkling with a little lemon juice. Serve with steamed rice and the Onion and Mint Relish.

Dry-fry the cloves, nutmeg, chilli, cumin and coriander in a heavy-based pan.

Bruschetta with Italian Beef

PREPARATION TIME: 40 minutes
TOTAL COOKING TIME: 20 minutes
SERVES 4

1 small red onion, finely chopped
400 g (12⅔ oz) lean beef mince
2 cloves garlic, crushed
⅓ cup (80 ml/2¾ fl oz) red wine
½ cup (125 ml/4 fl oz) chicken stock
2 teaspoons soft brown sugar
¼ cup (40 g/1⅓ oz) pitted Kalamata
   olives, chopped
1 tablespoon fresh oregano leaves
2 large tomatoes
150 g (4¾ oz) rocket, shredded
1 teaspoon balsamic vinegar
1 teaspoon extra virgin olive oil
1 loaf Italian bread, sliced diagonally into
   8 thick pieces
1 clove garlic, halved

1 Heat a little olive oil in a large frying pan and cook the onion over low heat until softened. Increase the heat to high, add the mince and brown well, breaking up any lumps with a fork or wooden spoon. Add the crushed garlic, red wine, stock, sugar and olives to the pan. Simmer for about 10 minutes, or until the liquid is reduced and the meat is tender. Stir in the oregano leaves and keep warm.

2 Chop the tomatoes into small pieces and toss with the shredded rocket, vinegar, olive oil and some salt and black pepper, to taste.

3 Toast the slices of bread on both sides and quickly rub with the clove of garlic. Spoon the beef over 4 slices of the bruschetta. On the other 4 slices, serve the tomato and rocket.

Using a long knife, slice the bread diagonally into 8 thick pieces.

Stir in the garlic, red wine, stock, sugar and chopped olives.

Combine the tomato and rocket and then toss in vinegar, oil and salt and pepper.

Olive Beef Balls with Tomato Sauce

PREPARATION TIME:
30 minutes + 30 minutes refrigeration
TOTAL COOKING TIME: 30 minutes
MAKES 30

600 g (1¼ lb) lean beef mince
1 cup (80 g/2⅔ oz) fresh breadcrumbs
1 egg, lightly beaten
30 stuffed green olives
fresh oregano sprigs, to garnish

Tomato Sauce
2 cloves garlic, crushed
425 g (13½ oz) can peeled tomatoes
45 g (1½ oz) can anchovy fillets in olive oil
2 tablespoons red wine

1 Mix together the beef mince, breadcrumbs, egg and some salt and pepper. Roll a level tablespoon of the mixture into a ball and then flatten to a disc about 1 cm (½ inch) thick. Place an olive on the meat and enclose it completely, rerolling to form a firm ball. Repeat with remaining mixture to make 30 balls. Refrigerate for at least 30 minutes.

2 Preheat the oven to moderate 180°C (350°F/Gas 4). Cover a large oven tray with foil, place the meatballs on it and bake for 20 minutes, turning once during cooking.

3 To make Tomato Sauce: Process all the ingredients in a food processor or blender until smooth. Pour into a small pan, bring to the boil and simmer over low heat for 10 minutes, stirring occasionally. Serve warm over the beef balls and garnish with a few oregano sprigs.

Note: To make fresh breadcrumbs, remove the crusts from day-old bread, break the bread into small pieces and then either rub between your hands or process in a food processor.

Press an olive onto each disc of meat and then roll the meat into a ball around it.

Put the meatballs on a foil-lined tray and bake, turning once during cooking.

Place all the Tomato Sauce ingredients in a food processor and blend until smooth.

Chicken Dumplings in Green Curry

PREPARATION TIME:
25 minutes + 2–3 hours refrigeration
TOTAL COOKING TIME: 35 minutes
SERVES 3–4

500 g (1 lb) chicken mince
3 spring onions, finely chopped
2 tablespoons small fresh coriander leaves
1 stem lemon grass, white part only,
  finely sliced
3 tablespoons fish sauce
1 teaspoon chicken stock powder
1½ cups (280 g/9 oz) cooked jasmine rice
1 egg, plus 1 egg white
2 teaspoons oil
2 tablespoons green curry paste
2 x 400 ml (12 ⅔ fl oz) cans coconut milk
4 fresh kaffir lime leaves
½ cup (25 g/¾ oz) fresh basil leaves
1 tablespoon lemon juice

1 Mix together the chicken mince, spring onion, coriander leaves, lemon grass, 2 tablespoons of the fish sauce, stock powder and some pepper. Add the rice and mix well with your hands.

2 In a separate bowl, beat the egg and egg white with electric beaters until thick and creamy and then fold into the chicken mixture. With lightly floured hands, roll tablespoons of the mixture into balls. Place on a tray, cover and refrigerate for 2–3 hours, or until firm.

3 Heat the oil in a large frying pan, add the green curry paste and stir over medium heat for 1 minute. Gradually stir in the coconut milk, then reduce the heat to simmer. Add the lime leaves and chicken dumplings to the sauce; cover and simmer for 25–30 minutes, stirring occasionally. Stir in the basil leaves, remaining fish sauce and lemon juice. Serve with steamed rice.

Beat the egg and egg white until thick and creamy.

Flour your hands and roll tablespoons of the mixture into balls.

When the sauce is simmering, add the lime leaves and chicken balls.

Beef and Kidney Bean Burrito Bake

PREPARATION TIME: 25 minutes
TOTAL COOKING TIME: 1 hour
SERVES 4

1 tablespoon oil
1 green chilli, seeded and finely chopped
1 red onion, chopped
500 g (1 lb) lean beef mince
420 g (13¼ oz) can kidney beans, drained
  and rinsed
425 g (13½ oz) can chopped tomatoes
450 g (14⅓ oz) can refried beans
½ teaspoon garam masala
1 teaspoon cumin seeds
4 x 30 cm (12 inch) flour tortillas
⅓ cup (90 g/3 oz) sour cream
135 g (4½ oz) Cheddar cheese, grated

1 Heat the oil in a large pan, add the green chilli and onion and stir for 1 minute. Increase the heat and add the beef mince. Cook for 4–5 minutes, or until the meat is just brown, breaking up any lumps with a fork or wooden spoon.

2 Stir in the kidney beans, tomatoes, refried beans, garam masala and cumin seeds. Reduce the heat and simmer gently for 25–30 minutes, stirring occasionally.

3 Preheat the oven to moderate 180°C (350°F/Gas 4). Divide the filling into 4 equal portions and spoon one portion down the centre of each tortilla. Then roll the tortilla up to enclose the filling.

4 Lightly brush a large ovenproof dish with melted butter or oil. Place the filled tortillas seam-side-down in the dish, spread evenly with the sour cream and sprinkle with Cheddar cheese. Bake for 20–25 minutes, or until the cheese has melted and started to brown and the burritos are slightly crispy. Serve immediately.

Add the mince to the chilli and onion and cook until lightly browned.

Stir in kidney beans, tomatoes, refried beans, garam masala and cumin seeds.

Spoon a line of filling down the centre of each of the tortillas.

Couscous with Moroccan Lamb

PREPARATION TIME: 30 minutes
TOTAL COOKING TIME: 50 minutes
SERVES 4

2 tablespoons olive oil
1 large onion, finely chopped
2 cloves garlic, finely chopped
½ teaspoon cumin seeds
1 teaspoon ground coriander
½ teaspoon ground cinnamon
¼ teaspoon ground nutmeg
500 g (1 lb) lamb mince
1 tablespoon chopped dried apricots
1 tablespoon raisins
2 tablespoons whole blanched almonds
½ cup (125 ml/4 fl oz) lamb or chicken stock
1 tablespoon honey
1 tablespoon finely chopped fresh parsley
300 g (9⅔ oz) couscous
2¼ cups (560 ml/18 fl oz) boiling water
2–3 tablespoons finely chopped fresh
  coriander

1 Heat 1 tablespoon of the oil in a large frying pan, add the onion and cook until soft and golden. Add the garlic, cumin, coriander, cinnamon and nutmeg to the pan and cook for 1 minute. Transfer the onion mixture to a plate. Heat the other tablespoon of oil in the same pan, add the lamb mince and stir until brown.

2 Return the onion and spices to the pan and add the apricots, raisins, almonds and combined stock and honey. Simmer for 40 minutes, allowing the stock to reduce. Season with salt and pepper, to taste, and stir in the parsley.

3 Just before serving, prepare the couscous by soaking in the boiling water for 5 minutes, or until all the water is absorbed. Season with salt. Top with the Moroccan Lamb and sprinkle with the chopped coriander.

Add garlic, cumin, coriander, cinnamon and nutmeg to the browned onion.

Mix apricots, raisins, almonds and the combined stock and honey into the mince.

Pour boiling water onto the couscous and leave to soak.

Savoury Filled Mushrooms

PREPARATION TIME: 20 minutes
TOTAL COOKING TIME: 20 minutes
SERVES 4

2 tablespoons olive oil
4 thin slices double smoked bacon,
   finely chopped
1 onion, finely chopped
⅓ cup (50 g/1⅔ oz) pine nuts
500 g (1 lb) finely ground pork and veal
   mince (see Note)
6 Kalamata olives, pitted and chopped
2 tablespoons chopped fresh parsley
2 teaspoons chopped fresh oregano
8 large mushrooms, stalks removed
1 cup (150 g/4¾ oz) finely grated
   mozzarella cheese

1 Preheat the oven to moderate 180°C (350°F/Gas 4). Lightly brush the base of an ovenproof dish with half the oil.

2 Heat the remaining oil in a frying pan, add the bacon, onion and pine nuts and stir for 3 minutes over low heat. Add the mince and olives and stir constantly until the mince is just browned, breaking up any large lumps of meat with a fork or wooden spoon. Do not overcook.

3 Stir the herbs through the meat mixture and season well with salt and pepper. Fill each mushroom cap with about 3 tablespoons of the filling and sprinkle with the cheese. Bake for 10 minutes.

Note: To grind the mince more finely, use a food processor or chop with a large, sharp knife.
Hint: Delicious eaten hot or cold with a green salad and crusty bread.

The mince can be ground up more finely using a large cook's knife.

Add mince and olives to the mixture and stir constantly until the mince is browned.

Fill each mushroom cap with about 3 tablespoons of the filling.

Lemon Grass Prawn Satays

PREPARATION TIME:
20 minutes + 1 hour refrigeration
TOTAL COOKING TIME: 15 minutes
SERVES 6

1 tablespoon oil
1 clove garlic, crushed
1 tablespoon grated fresh ginger
1 tablespoon finely chopped lemon grass,
   white part only
1 onion, finely chopped
1 tablespoon tandoori curry paste
4 kaffir lime leaves, finely shredded
1 tablespoon coconut cream
2 teaspoons grated lime rind
600 g (1¼ lb) medium raw prawns, peeled
   and deveined
3 stems lemon grass, cut into 15 cm (6 inch)
   lengths

1 Heat the oil in a frying pan, add the garlic, ginger, lemon grass and onion and cook over medium heat for 3 minutes, or until golden.

2 Add the tandoori paste and kaffir lime leaves to the pan and cook for 5 minutes, or until the tandoori paste is fragrant. Allow to cool slightly. Transfer the mixture to a food processor, add the coconut cream, lime rind and prawns and process until finely minced. Divide the mixture into 6 portions and shape around the lemon grass stems with wet hands, leaving about 3 cm (1¼ inches) uncovered at each end of the stems. The mixture is quite soft, so take care when handling it. Using wet hands will make the mixture easier to manage. Refrigerate for 1 hour.

3 Cook the satays under a preheated medium grill for 5 minutes, or until cooked through.

Add the tandoori paste and kaffir lime leaves to the pan and cook until fragrant.

Transfer the mixture to a food processor; add coconut cream, lime zest and prawns.

Wet your hands to make handling easier and shape the mixture around the stems.

Burritos

PREPARATION TIME: 15 minutes
TOTAL COOKING TIME: 40 minutes
SERVES 2–4

1–2 tablespoons olive oil
1 large onion, finely sliced
500 g (1 lb) lean beef mince
1 cinnamon stick
1 bay leaf
4 whole cloves
2 cups (500 ml/16 fl oz) beef stock
2 teaspoons soft brown sugar
tortillas, for serving

Tomato Salsa
1 tomato, finely chopped
1 red onion, finely sliced
2–3 tablespoons chopped fresh coriander
3 tablespoons lemon juice
2 teaspoons grated lemon rind

1 Heat the oil in a large heavy-based pan. Add the onion and cook over medium heat until golden. Add the beef mince, cinnamon stick, bay leaf, cloves, stock and sugar. Bring the mixture to the boil, reduce the heat and simmer for 30 minutes, or until the mince is soft and has absorbed almost all the liquid. Stir the mince regularly and break up any lumps with a fork or wooden spoon.

2 To make Tomato Salsa: Thoroughly mix all the ingredients in a small bowl.

3 Remove the cinnamon stick, bay leaf and cloves from the mince mixture. Use 2 forks to break the mince up finely. Serve rolled up in a tortilla with the Tomato Salsa.

Note: The mince mixture can be made up to 3 days in advance. Cover with plastic wrap and refrigerate. The salsa can be made several hours in advance. Use flour or corn tortillas.

Add the mince, cinnamon stick, bay leaf, cloves, stock and sugar to the onion.

Simmer until the mince is soft and has absorbed almost all the liquid.

Remove the cinnamon stick, bay leaf and cloves from the mince.

Prosciutto, Veal and Apricot Pate

PREPARATION TIME:
20 minutes + 3–4 hours refrigeration
TOTAL COOKING TIME: 45 minutes
SERVES 4

8 slices prosciutto
150 g (4 ¾ oz) chicken livers
350 g (11¼ oz) pork and veal mince
1 small onion, chopped
100 g (3⅓ oz) dried apricots, chopped
250 g (8 oz) baby English spinach leaves,
   washed and dried
1 tablespoon finely chopped fresh rosemary
1 egg, lightly beaten
1 teaspoon seeded mustard
1 tablespoon plain flour
60 g (2 oz) pistachio nuts, shelled
   and chopped

1 Grease four 1-cup (250 ml/8 fl oz) capacity ovenproof moulds and line each with 2 slices of prosciutto. Preheat the oven to moderate 180°C (350°F/Gas 4).

2 Process the chicken livers, pork and veal mince, onion, apricots and spinach in a food processor. Transfer to a bowl and stir in the rosemary, egg, mustard, flour, pistachio nuts and some black pepper.

3 Press the mixture into the moulds, fold the prosciutto over and cover with greased foil. Stand the moulds in a baking dish and pour in enough water to come halfway up their sides. Bake for 40–45 minutes. Remove from the oven and water bath and refrigerate for at least 3–4 hours.

Lightly grease each mould and line with 2 overlapping slices of prosciutto.

Spoon the mixture into the moulds and fold the prosciutto ends over the top.

Pour enough water into the dish to come halfway up the sides of the moulds.

Gourmet Veal Sausage Roll

PREPARATION TIME: 20 minutes

TOTAL COOKING TIME: 45 minutes

SERVES 4

500 g (1 lb) veal mince
1 onion, finely chopped
2 tablespoons tomato paste
½ cup (40 g/1⅓ oz) fresh breadcrumbs
200 g (6½ oz) fresh ricotta
¼ cup (45 g/1½ oz) Kalamata olives, pitted
  and chopped
½ cup (75 g/2½ oz) sun-dried tomatoes,
  chopped
1 tablespoon shredded fresh basil
1 sheet ready-rolled puffpastry
1 egg, lightly beaten

1 Preheat the oven to moderately hot 200°C (400°F/Gas 6). Mix together in a bowl the veal mince, onion, tomato paste and breadcrumbs.

2 Spread the mixture onto a large piece of foil to form a 25 cm (10 inch) square. Then spread the ricotta evenly over the mince square and top with the Kalamata olives, sun-dried tomato and basil. Roll up the mince square like a Swiss roll, removing the foil as you go. Place the roll onto one end of the sheet of puff pastry and roll up the pastry to encase the mince roll, trimming any overhanging edges.

3 Place the pastry seam-side-down on a non-stick baking tray. Using a sharp knife, cut several steam holes in the top of the pastry. Brush lightly with the beaten egg and bake for 45 minutes, or until the pastry is golden and the sausage roll is cooked through. Pour off any juices before serving.

Scatter the olives, sun-dried tomato and basil over the ricotta.

Roll up the puff pastry sheet to enclose the mince.

Score the top of the pastry several times with a sharp knife to make steam holes.

Prawn-filled Baby Eggplants

PREPARATION TIME: 15 minutes
TOTAL COOKING TIME: 35 minutes
SERVES 4 as a first course

300 g (9⅔ oz) raw prawns
50 g (1⅔ oz) butter
8 slender eggplants
2 cloves garlic, crushed
1 onion, finely chopped
1 large tomato, chopped
1 tablespoon tomato paste
¼ cup (60 ml/2 fl oz) white wine

1 Preheat the oven to moderate 180°C (350°F/Gas 4). Peel the prawns, and devein. Then chop the meat until it is finely minced.

2 Melt the butter in a frying pan, add the eggplants and cook in batches over medium heat for 5 minutes, or until soft. Remove and drain well on paper towels.

3 Add the garlic and onion to the pan and cook for 5 minutes, or until the onion is golden. Stir in the chopped tomato and prawn mince and cook for 3 minutes.

4 Cut the eggplants in half lengthways and place in a baking dish. Spoon the tomato and prawn mixture over the eggplants. In a small bowl, stir the tomato paste and white wine until combined and then pour it over the top. Bake for 20 minutes and serve immediately.

Hint: Eggplants become fairly soft when cooked, so use a very sharp knife to cut them in half to prevent squashing them.

Chop the prawns with a sharp cook's knife until they are finely minced.

Melt the butter and cook the baby eggplants in batches until soft.

Place the eggplant halves in a baking dish and spoon the mixture on top.

Turkey Burgers with Cranberry Sauce

PREPARATION TIME: 30–40 minutes
TOTAL COOKING TIME: 20 minutes
SERVES 4

Cranberry Sauce
30 g (1 oz) butter
½ small onion, finely chopped
2 teaspoons soft brown sugar
¼ teaspoon mixed spice
½ teaspoon ground ginger
2 teaspoons grated lime rind
1 teaspoon balsamic vinegar
4 tablespoons cranberry sauce

500 g (1 lb) turkey breast fillets
2 tablespoons finely chopped fresh chives
1 egg, lightly beaten
⅔ cup (55 g/1¾ oz) fresh breadcrumbs
2 cloves garlic, crushed

1 To make Cranberry Sauce: Heat the butter in a pan, add the onion and cook for 3–4 minutes, or until soft. Stir in the sugar, spice and ginger and cook for 1 minute. Add the lime rind, vinegar and cranberry sauce and simmer gently for 3 minutes. Remove from the heat and cool slightly.

2 Trim the turkey of excess fat and sinew, chop roughly and mince in a food processor for 20–30 seconds. Transfer to a large bowl and add the chives, egg, breadcrumbs, garlic and some salt and pepper. Mix with your hands until well combined. With wet hands, divide the mixture into patties.

3 Heat a little oil and butter in a large heavy-based frying pan. Cook the patties, in batches if necessary, for 3–4 minutes each side, or until golden. Drain on paper towels. Serve with the Cranberry Sauce.

Chop up the chives finely, using a very sharp knife.

Add the lime rind, vinegar and cranberry sauce to the mixture and simmer gently.

Cook the patties in butter and oil until golden on both sides and cooked through.

Chicken Teriyaki Packages

PREPARATION TIME: 50 minutes + soaking
TOTAL COOKING TIME: 25 minutes
MAKES 24

5 Chinese dried mushrooms
1 tablespoon vegetable oil
2 cloves garlic, crushed
1 teaspoon finely grated ginger
350 g (11¼ oz) chicken mince
1 small leek, finely sliced
1 tablespoon soy sauce
2 tablespoons dry sherry
1 tablespoon sake
1 tablespoon white sugar
1–2 teaspoons chilli sauce
100 g (3⅓ oz) fresh rice noodles,
    finely sliced
15 sheets filo pastry
90 g (3 oz) butter, melted
2 tablespoons sesame seeds

1 Place the mushrooms in a bowl, pour on boiling water and soak for 30 minutes. Drain and chop finely. Heat the oil in a large pan, add the garlic, ginger, chicken mince and leek and stir-fry for 4–5 minutes. Then mix in the soy sauce, sherry, sake, sugar and chilli sauce. Fold in the mushrooms and rice noodles and remove the mixture from the heat. Preheat the oven to moderate 180°C (350°F/Gas 4).

2 Unfold the filo, remove 1 sheet and cover the rest with a damp tea towel to prevent them from drying out. Brush the sheet of filo lightly with melted butter. Top with another 2 sheets, brushing each with butter. Cut crossways into 7 cm (2¾ inch) strips and spoon 1 tablespoon of the filling onto one end of each strip. Fold the ends over to form a triangle and continue folding to the end of each strip. Repeat with the remaining pastry and filling.

3 Place the triangles on a lightly oiled baking tray, brush with melted butter and sprinkle with sesame seeds. Bake for 12–15 minutes, or until a light golden brown.

Fold in the mushrooms and rice noodles and remove the mixture from the heat.

Place 3 lightly buttered filo sheets on top of each other and cut into strips.

Fold ends over filling to form a triangle and keep folding to the end of the strip.

Meatballs with Fusilli

PREPARATION TIME: 25 minutes
TOTAL COOKING TIME: 35 minutes
SERVES 6

3–4 slices white bread
750 g (1½ lb) pork and veal mince or lean
 beef mince
1 onion, finely chopped
2 tablespoons choppedfresh parsley
1 egg, beaten
rind and juice of half a lemon
¼ cup (25 g/ ¾ oz) freshly grated Parmesan
2 cloves garlic, crushed
¼ cup (30 g/1 oz) plain flour
2 tablespoons olive oil
425 g (13½ oz) can crushed tomatoes
½ cup (125 ml/4 fl oz) beef stock
½ cup (125 ml/4 fl oz) red wine
2 tablespoons chopped fresh basil
500 g (1 lb) fusilli

1 Process the bread in a food processor to form breadcrumbs. Using your hands, combine with the mince, onion, parsley, egg, lemon rind and juice, Parmesan, half the garlic and some salt and pepper in a bowl. Roll tablespoons of the mixture into balls and roll in the seasoned flour.

2 Heat the oil in a frying pan and cook the balls in batches until golden. Remove and drain on paper towels. Drain the excess fat from the pan.

3 Add the tomatoes, stock, wine, basil, the remaining garlic and salt and pepper to the frying pan and bring to the boil.

4 Reduce the heat, return the meatballs to the pan and simmer for 10–15 minutes. Cook the fusilli in boiling water until just tender and drain. Serve with the meatballs.

Combine the ingredients for meatballs in a bowl and use your hands to mix well.

When the meatballs are browned, remove from the pan and drain on paper towels.

Pour the fusilli into a large pan of rapidly boiling water.

Savoury Beef Gougere

PREPARATION TIME: 1 hour
TOTAL COOKING TIME: 1 hour 20 minutes
SERVES 4

1 tablespoon oil
1 onion, finely chopped
400 g (12⅔ oz) beef mince
1 celery stick, finely sliced
1 small carrot, finely sliced
90 g (3 oz) mushrooms, sliced
2 tablespoons chopped fresh parsley
1 tablespoon plain flour
¾ cup (185 ml/6 fl oz) beef stock
2 tablespoons mango chutney
2 tablespoons fresh breadcrumbs

Cheese Choux Pastry
1 cup (250 ml/8 fl oz) water
100 g (3⅓ oz) butter
1 cup (125 g/4 oz) plain flour
4 eggs, beaten
1 cup (160 g/5¼ oz) cubed Cheddar cheese

1 Heat the oil in a frying pan, add the onion and cook until soft. Add the mince and brown over high heat, breaking up any lumps with a fork. Mix in the celery, carrot, mushroom and parsley and cook for 1 minute. Stir in the flour and cook for another minute. Remove from the heat and stir in the stock and chutney. Return to the heat and simmer, covered, for about 30 minutes, stirring occasionally. Add a little water if it starts to stick to the bottom. Season, to taste.

2 To make Cheese Choux Pastry: Stir water and butter in a pan until the butter has melted; bring to the boil. As soon as the liquid begins to boil, add the sifted flour and beat well. The mixture will become very smooth and leave the sides of the pan. Cool slightly. Transfer mixture to a food processor or small bowl and gradually add the egg, beating or processing well after each addition, until the mixture is stiff and glossy. Season with salt and stir in the cheese.

3 Preheat the oven to moderately hot 200°C (400°F/Gas 6). Lightly oil a large ovenproof dish, about 25 cm (10 inches) long, and spoon the pastry around the edge in a thick border. Spoon in the filling and sprinkle with breadcrumbs. Bake for 40 minutes, or until the pastry is puffed and golden.

For the Choux Pastry, beat the sifted flour into the boiling water and butter.

Transfer the mixture to a small bowl, add the egg gradually and beat it in well.

Spicy Lamb Pie

PREPARATION TIME: 40 minutes
TOTAL COOKING TIME: 1 hour 15 minutes
SERVES 6

1 tablespoon oil
1 large onion, chopped
2 cloves garlic, crushed
500 g (1 lb) lamb mince
1 teaspoon ground cinnamon
2 teaspoons ground cumin
1 teaspoon curry powder
¼ cup (60 ml/2 fl oz) red wine
¼ cup (60 g/2 oz) tomato paste
⅓ cup (50 g/1⅔ oz) currants
500 g (1 lb) English spinach leaves, shredded
2 tablespoons marmalade
¼ cup (60 ml/2 fl oz) beef stock
12 sheets filo pastry
80 g (2⅔ oz) butter, melted

1 Preheat the oven to moderate 180°C (350°F/Gas 4). Brush a 21 cm (8½ inch) round pie dish with butter. Heat the oil in a pan, add the onion and garlic and stir for 2 minutes. Add the lamb mince and stir for 5 minutes, breaking up any lumps with a fork.

2 Add the spices, wine, tomato paste, currants, spinach, marmalade and stock. Simmer, uncovered, for 20 minutes, or until all the liquid has evaporated. Season with salt and pepper. Allow to cool.

3 Remove 1 sheet of pastry and cover the rest with a damp tea towel to prevent drying out. Brush the sheet of filo lightly with the butter and cover with another 2 sheets, brushing each with butter. Cut in half, crossways, and line the pie dish with the 2 halves of pastry, leaving any overhanging edges. Spoon the lamb mixture into the dish. Brush the remaining sheets of pastry with butter, scrunch each into a ball and place on top of the pie. Bake for 45 minutes, or until the pastry turns golden.

Add the spices, red wine, tomato paste, currants, spinach, marmalade and stock.

Cut the 3-layered sheet of filo pastry in half and line a pie dish with the 2 halves.

Scrunch the remaining 9 filo sheets into balls and place on top of the pie.

All our recipes are thoroughly tested in a specially developed test kitchen. Standard metric measuring cups and spoons are used in the development of our recipes. All cup and spoon measurements are level. We have used 60 g (2¼ oz/Grade 3) eggs in all recipes. Sizes of cans vary from manufacturer to manufacturer and between countries – use the can size closest to the one suggested in the recipe.

CONVERSION GUIDE

1 cup = 250 ml (9 fl oz)

1 teaspoon = 5 ml

1 Australian tablespoon = 20 ml (4 teaspoons)

1 UK/US tablespoon = 15 ml (3 teaspoons)

Where temperature ranges are indicated, the lower figure applies to gas ovens, the higher to electric ovens. This allows for the fact that the flame in gas ovens generates a drier heat, which effectively cooks food faster than the moister heat of an electric oven, even if the temperature setting is the same.

DRY MEASURES	LIQUID MEASURES	LINEAR MEASURES
30 g = 1 oz	30 ml = 1 fl oz	6 mm = ¼ inch
250 g = 9 oz	125 ml = 4 fl oz	1 cm = ½ inch
500 g = 1 lb 2 oz	250 ml = 9 fl oz	2.5 cm = 1 inch

	°C	°F	GAS MARK
Very slow	120	250	½
Slow	150	300	2
Mod slow	160	325	3
Moderate	180	350	4
Mod hot	190(g)–210(e)	375–425	5
Hot	200(g)–240(e)	400–475	6
Very hot	230(g)–260(e)	450–525	8

CUP CONVERSIONS – DRY INGREDIENTS

1 cup almonds, slivered whole = 125 g (4½ oz)

1 cup cheese, lightly packed processed cheddar = 155 g (5½ oz)

1 cup wheat flour = 125 g (4½ oz)

1 cup wholemeal flour = 140 g (5 oz)

1 cup minced (ground) meat = 250 g (9 oz)

1 cup pasta shapes = 125 g (4½ oz)

1 cup raisins = 170 g (6 oz)

1 cup rice, short grain, raw = 200 g (7 oz)

1 cup sesame seeds = 160 g (6 oz)

1 cup split peas = 250 g (9 oz)

(g) = gas (e) = electric

Note: For fan-forced ovens, check your appliance manual, but as a general rule, set the oven temperature to 20°C lower than the temperature indicated in the recipe.

INTERNATIONAL GLOSSARY

capsicum	sweet bell pepper	cornflour	cornstarch
chick pea	garbanzo bean	eggplant	aubergine
chilli	chile, chili pepper	spring onion	scallion
		zucchini	courgette

Murdoch Books Pty Limited

Erico House, 6th Floor North, 93-99 Upper Richmond Road, Putney, London, SW15 2TG, United Kingdom.

This edition published in 2007 for INDEX: Garrard Way, Kettering, NN16 8TD, United Kingdom.

ISBN-13: 978 1 921259 68 5   ISBN-10: 1 921259 68 X

Printed by Sing Cheong Printing Co. Ltd. PRINTED IN CHINA.